Home Science Experiments for Smart Kids!

65+ Fun and Educational Science Projects for Children to Learn How to Become a Water Bender, Create Slime in A Cup, Make Homemade Ice Cream and So Much More (KidsVille Books)

Lisa Watts

This book belongs to this Scientist:

_____

Table of Contents

SPECIAL BONUS!

Want These 2 Bonus Books for <u>free</u>?

Get <u>FREE</u>, unlimited access to these and all of our new books by joining the KidsVille Books Facebook group!

SCAN W/ YOUR CAMERA TO JOIN!

PLUS! Get entered into our monthly $20 Amazon Gift card Giveaway

Introduction

Science is an essential part of the everyday life. Biology makes us, chemistry makes new things, physics helps us move around and there is so much more each category of science does for us humans. Needless to say, without the knowledge of science, we would be unable to perform simple everyday activities such as cooking, moving and even eating and sleeping! Therefore, it is important we learn from science and what better way to learn than to indulge ourselves into it. This book focuses on General science and helps you conduct experiments using everyday equipment. They are all based on simple scientific principles without which the world would be a mess. Each experiment will help you learn something knew about for e.g.; how water works, what different densities mean, how different molecules react to one another, in what conditions certain things expand or contract and much more.

How to use this book

There are a few things that need to be kept in mind whilst going ahead with the experiments.

Here are a few guidelines for the use of the following book:

1. Read each experiment thoroughly and have it read by your adult supervisor.

2. Keep the book close to you at all times whilst performing an experiment from it.

3. Once you began performing an experiment, remember to follow the instructions strictly.

4. Be very cautious of the proportions of different ingredients involved in the experiment. Proportions need to be exact.

5. The book has tried and tested experiments, therefore, do not make any modifications whatsoever to your experiments.

6. This book is meant for children over the age of 6. Keep away from younger children.

7. Use the lines provided after each experiment to document how your experiment went.

The 5 steps of the Scientific Method

The scientific method is a type of experimentation that is normally used to understand certain observations and then answer questions that arise from those observations.

Most scientists use the mentioned series of steps to conduct their experiments, however, modifications may take place to better suit who the scientist is and what the experiment is. So, whether you are in a classroom setting, competing in a science competition or just at home bored, going through these steps and understanding them will help you conduct your experiments in the best way possible and help you learn from them as well.

1. Ask a Question/s

The first thing to do is ask a question; How, What, When, Who, Which, Why, or Where?

2. Do prior Research

Before you dive into the experiment itself, research on how it works and what you should expect.

3. A Hypothesis

Any experiment requires a Hypothesis. This being an assumption of what will come out of the experiment.

4. Test Your Hypothesis

Now this is the most exciting part. The experiment itself!

5. Analysis of the data and coming up with a conclusion

Once you're done with the experiment, you'll see the results and form a conclusion. This could be that whether your hypothesis was supported by the experiment or not.

A glass full of storms

Do you ever wonder, on a hot summer day, what it would be like to have a storm? And, does your dad shave? You may ask what the correlation to those two is. It's simple. In this experiment we'll learn to create a storm of our own using shaving cream!

Things you'll need:

- A big glass
- Water
- Food coloring
- A spoon
- And finally, some shaving cream!

Procedure:

Step 1: Get half a glass of water.

Step 2: Put shaving cream atop the water to almost fill the glass. (Leave some space empty)

Step 3: Flatten the top of the shaving cream using a spoon.

Step 4: Now fill half a glass of water, add food coloring to it.

Step 5: Slowly start adding spoonful of the colored water.

Step 6: Watch as the shaving cream cloud gets heavy and starts to precipitate the colored water.

But how does it work?

Water can be stored into clouds. For this experiment, shaving cream is our cloud since it too, can hold water molecules. After a while, the clouds reach their limit and get very heavy. When this happens, they start to release droplets of rain. The same happens with the shaving cream!

Precautions for your safety:

- Do not use hot water in the experiment.
- Do not ingest the food coloring used in the experiment.
- Use a clear plastic cup rather than a glass.
- Perform the experiment under adult supervision.

Become a water bender

Most of us have watched Avatar: the last Air bender. We see Aang bend air with no problem, and sometimes we might get jealous. Here's the perfect solution to be a bender yourself, but of water! You will use electricity to bend water, isn't that even better?

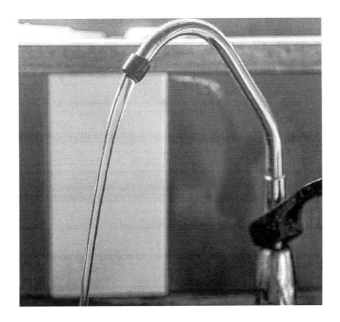

Things you'll need:

- A bathroom/kitchen tap
- A plastic comb
- Your hair! But completely dried.

Procedure:

Step 1:   Pick up your plastic comb and gently start brushing it through your hair, increasing pace slowly, until you've done it about 15 times.

Step 2: Turn on the tap and gradually turn it down till there's very little water coming out from the tap.

Step 3: Now take your plastic comb and bring it in close proximity to the water stream.

Step 4: You will notice that the water stream starts to bend towards your comb. You might move it around slowly and notice the water following you! You've now officially become a water bender.

How it works:

Brushing your hair leads to tiny electrons being collected onto your comb. These particles have a negative charge. We know that things with a negative charge attract those with positive charges. Now, the water from the tap has a positive charge and that is why the comb will attract the water towards itself. This simple science experiment will not only let you become a superhero like Aang! but also help you understand the science behind electricity.

Precautions for your safety:

- Do not use a metal comb that may hurt you.
- Keep the tap water at its cool or normal setting, do not set it too hot.
- Do not brush your hair aggressively.
- Perform the experiment under adult supervision.

Inflate your balloon with yeast

Blowing tens of balloons for a birthday party might become a redundant and boring activity. But don't worry, there's a way to spice it up! You can use yeast to inflate your balloons!

Things you'll need:

- A clear and clean plastic bottle
- Warm water
- Yeast from a local grocery store
- A heaped teaspoon of sugar
- A balloon

Procedure:

Step 1: Fill the bottle with approximately 1.5 inch of warm water.

Step 2: Add in the yeast and gently shake the bottle for some time until it dissolves.

Step 3: Now add sugar to the mixture and shake and swirl it again.

Step 4: Blow the balloon a tiny bit and place it onto the bottle's neck.

Step 5: Place the bottle in a warm area, like near a sunny window or a closed off cabinet.

You will see that the balloon starts to inflate atop the bottle!

How it works:

Cold/dry yeast is resting and so it is inactive. Once dissolved in water it becomes alive! Like any other living thing yeast requires food for energy. That is why we add sugar to the yeast mixture, its food for the yeast. When the yeast eats the sugar, it releases a gas called carbon dioxide. When enough carbon dioxide is produced it starts to fill up the bottle and the balloon.

Precautions for your safety:

- Do not ingest the yeast.
- Do not use a glass bottle.
- Add the warm water to the bottle wearing insulating gloves to avoid any burns.
- If not available, ask an adult to help you pour the water into the bottle.

Egg down the bottle

Do you ever eat too much and are left with an uneaten hardboiled egg? Do you feel the need to put it in a bottle? Probably not. But hey! Wouldn't it be interesting seeing a large egg make its way down the thin neck of a bottle? The following experiment is about making an egg move on its own into a bottle.

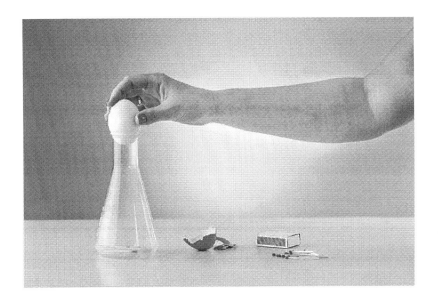

Things you'll need:

- Hardboiled egg (the shell should be removed)
- Glass bottle
- Piece of paper (thick)
- Lighter/match

The procedure:

Step 1: The egg should be placed near bottle so that you can put the egg on the bottle quickly.

Step 2: Take a thick piece of paper.

Step 3: Use your lighter/match to light the piece of paper.

Step 4: While the paper is burning, put it in to the glass bottle with caution.

Step 5: Immediately after putting the paper in, Put the egg on top of the bottle.

Step 6: Now you can see how the egg slowly moves into the bottle!

How it works:

It all comes down to the air pressure, in the start the air pressure inside and outside the bottle was the same. The air inside the bottle started to heat up and expand after placing the burning paper. After placing the egg, the paper stopped burning which caused the air inside the glass bottle to cool down as well as contract. The contraction of air caused there to be less pressure inside the bottle than outside. The egg was able to go down the bottle because the higher air pressure pushed it down.

Precautions for your safety:

- Ask an adult to boil the egg for you.
- Do **NOT** burn the paper yourself, ask an adult to do it for you.
- The paper should be placed into the bottle with extreme caution.

- Conduct the experiment strictly understand adult supervision.

The Lava Lamp

Have you ever walked past a gift store and wished you could get one of those fancy Lava Lamps? But you did not because either they were too expensive or too fragile. Well here is a cool way to make one at home! And guess what? It won't cost you a penny or be easily breakable.

Your Lava Lamp will be based on the properties of water and oil. Both of which have different sized molecules making them immiscible (They do not mix together).

Things you'll need:

- Vegetable oil
- Water

- Food colouring
- A clear plastic bottle/jar
- Finally, some Alka Seltzer tablets

The procedure:

Step 1: You have to begin by adding ¼ litres of water to your plastic bottle.

Step 2: Then add the vegetable oil into the bottle until it is almost full.

Step 3: Wait a few minutes so that the oil and water have time to separate.

Step 4: Add the food coloring of your preference to bring a burst of color!

Step 5: Lastly to complete your lamp break your alka seltzer into half and then add part of into your plastic bottle!

You will see that the oil and water do not mix together, and the food coloring sinks to the bottom coming up in form of colorful blobs. We're all done, here's your lava lamp!

How it works:

The water and oil do not mix because the oil is less dense and lighter than water. The oil does not mix with food coloring either because of it being water soluble and the fizzy tablet which is Alka Seltzer reacts with the water to create bubbles made of carbon dioxide which attach themselves to the blobs of colored water. When the bubbles come out of the blobs, the water becomes heavy and sinks back down. This cycle is repeated over and over again until the fizzy tablet is fully dissolved.

Precautions for your safety:

- Do not ingest the alka seltzer tablet.
- Do not use hot water.
- Do not ingest food colouring.
- Conduct the experiment in the presence of an adult.

Your own parachute

It is always interesting to look at professionals use parachutes. Flying and landing from such high lengths yet without any harm. In this experiment, we'll make a parachute of our own, of course one that we will **not** be able to use but to understand how an actual parachute works.

Things you'll need:

- String
- Some type of light material (preferably a plastic bag)
- Cutter or scissors
- One of your action figures/dolls to act as your human weight!

Procedure:

Step 1: Cut a large square out of the light material of choice and turn it into an octagon.

Step 2: Punch a hole in each edge of the octagon.

Step 3: Now attach the same size of string in each of the holes.

Step 4: Put your object in the middle under the light material.

Step 5: Now take each of the string and tie it to your doll/action figure.

Step 6: Gently drop the parachute from a higher point, like a chair and for greater impact, from your terrace if you have one.

How it works:

The mechanics are simple. As you drop the parachute and the weight of the figure acts on it; that and large surface area of your used material cause air resistance. This resistance is what will cause your parachute to land slowly and safely.

Precautions for your safety:

- Get child safe scissors or ask an adult to cut the holes for you.
- If you drop the parachute from your terrace, make sure an adult is with you.
- Perform the experiment under adult supervision.

Tornado in a bottle

The following experiment is about creating your own tornado, one that is a lot smaller and a lot less dangerous than the ones you see outside!

Things you'll need:

- Clear plastic bottle (with a cap)
- Glitter
- Water
- Dish washing liquid

The procedure:

Step 1: Pour water into the plastic bottle until it is 3 quarters full.

Step 2:   Put in a few drops of the dish washing liquid.

Step 3:   Add some glitter to make the tornado easier to see.

Step 4:   Put the cap on.

Step 5:   Flip the plastic bottle upside down and hold it by the neck.

Step 6:   Spin the bottle in a circular motion very quickly. After a few seconds, stop and you'll see a mini tornado forming. (This will take a few tries to work)

How it works:

By spinning the bottle, a water vortex is formed which looks like a tornado. Centripetal force which is an inward force that directs an object or fluid which in this case is water towards the center of its circular path, is the reason why the water is spinning around the centre of the vortex.

Precautions:

Do not use hot water.
Do not ingest dish washing liquid.
Do not ingest glitter.
Conduct the experiment in the presence of an adult.

Massive expanding soap

This expanding ivory soap will leave kids amazed and wanting some more of this magic which is both clean and safe!

Things you'll need:

- Ivory soap
- Large microwave safe bowl
- A microwave oven of course!

The procedure:

Step 1: Place the bar of ivory soap into the bowl.

Step 2: Microwave it for 2 minutes on high power.

Step 3: It will start to grow large.

Step 4: Wait for a few minutes as both the bowl and the foam cool down.

How it works:

Ivory soap has many little air bubbles in it so when the soap gets heated in the microwave, the air bubbles start to get bigger. The soap will stay expanded (when it cools down it will shrink only a little) since it is a solid.

Precautions:

Be careful when using the microwave.
Do not touch the soap when it is hot.
Do not ingest the soap.
Conduct the experiment in the presence of an adult.

Elephant Toothpaste

Playing with foam in the shower can't be enough sometimes. Here's a way to make giant amounts of fluffy foam through performing an exothermic reaction!

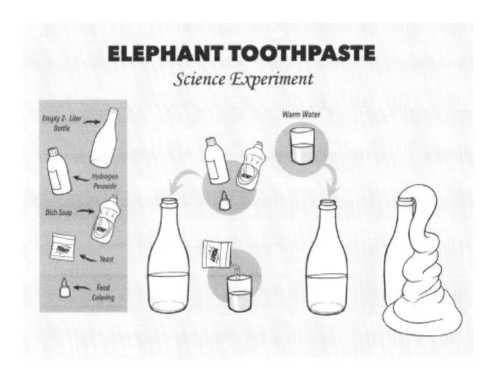

What you'll need:

- A glass/cup
- Dish washing liquid
- 473 ML Soda bottle (empty)
- 20 Volume hydrogen peroxide
- One packet of yeast

- Around 15-20 mls of warmed water
- Liquid food color
- Funnel
- Safety eye gear

Procedure:

Step 1: Add approximately half a cup of hydrogen peroxide liquid into your soda bottle.

Step 2: Put some 15 drops of vibrant food coloring.

Step 3: Add in a tablespoon of dish washing liquid and gently shake the bottle.

Step 4: Set aside your bottle for now.

Step 5: Take another empty cup and add the water and yeast in it. Stir the mixture till it becomes thicker.

Step 6: Place the funnel atop the bottle you had set aside.

Step 7: Here is the part we all have been waiting for! Pour the yeast mixture into the soda bottle and watch as the foam starts to develop.

How it works:

The foam bubbles are filled with oxygen. Yeast acts as the catalyst increasing the speed of the process. It then breaks away the oxygen from the hydrogen peroxide. Since this happens in basically the wink of an eye, lots and lots of bubbles are created. What you performed is an exothermic reaction which is why your bottle should become warm. This happens because an exothermic reaction releases heat. The foam is merely oxygen, water and soap.

LISA WATTS

Precautions for your safety:

- Do not handle the hydrogen peroxide yourself. Get an adult to do it for you.
- Do not touch/ingest the foam.
- Do not consume the yeast or food coloring.
- Handle warm water with extreme precaution.

Hot ice

We're all familiar with ice that's cold but did you know ice can be hot too? And that you can make it at home?!

Things you'll need:

- Baking soda
- Vinegar
- Measuring cup
- Saucepan
- Jar
- Plastic tray

The procedure:

Step 1: Measure and pour 4 cups of vinegar into a saucepan.

Step 2: Slowly add 4 tablespoons of baking soda into the vinegar. The mixture should fizz as you have now created sodium acetate.

Step 3: Boil this solution over low heat for about an hour or until small crystals form on the edge of the saucepan.

Step 4: Scrape the crystals from the side of the pan into a plastic tray.

Step 5: Transfer the hot mixture left in the saucepan into a jar and leave it in a freezer for 20 minutes for it to cool down.

Step 6: After taking the cool solution out of the freezer pour it over the crystals in the plastic tray a little at a time. The solution should start solidifying and turning into ice which is hot to the touch.

How it works:

Combining the baking soda and vinegar creates sodium acetate which contains water within it. When this mixture is boiled the water slowly evaporates and decreases in amount though it does not completely finish due to which the solution remains a liquid and does not solidify into crystals (except those formed at the edge of the pan) as the water molecules do not allow the sodium acetate molecules to form crystals. When this solution is put in the freezer it becomes supercooled which means that the temperature drops below its freezing point and causes it to remain a liquid rather than turning into a solid. The few crystals that the liquid is poured over act as a nucleation site meaning they assist to change the state of the solution from liquid to solid and this change of state called crystallization produces heat making it feel hot to the touch.

Precautions:

- Ask an adult to handle the boiling portion of the experiment.
- Do not ingest baking soda.
- Do not ingest the sodium acetate solution made.
- Conduct the experiment under adult supervision.

Lemon volcano

If you like the traditional volcano experiment but are bored with its simplicity, try the lemon volcano experiment which is not only more fun but is also more visibly attractive along with

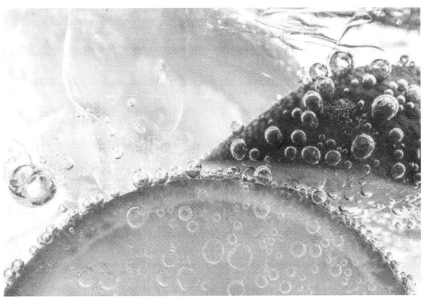

yummy smelling.

Things you'll need:

- Lemons
- Food coloring
- Baking soda
- Knife
- Dish soap
- Wooden craft stick
- Plastic tray

- Jar

The procedure:

Step 1: Place your lemon on a plastic tray after cutting it flat at the base to make it stand upright.

Step 2: From the top to the center cut out an inverted cone shape. The leftover lemon is now the structure of the volcano.

Step 3: Take a wooden craft stick and squish the inside of the lemon on the plastic tray to release the juices from inside.

Step 4: Add a few drops of food coloring in the middle of the lemon along with some dish soap to make the foaming more exciting.

Step 5: Put a tablespoon of baking soda in the lemon.

Step 6: Mix the lemon juice, baking soda, dish soap and food coloring inside the lemon with the wooden stick for the reaction to happen. You will see fizzing and foaming from the lemon.

How it works:

The citric acid contained in the lemon reacts with baking soda also known as sodium bicarbonate to give off carbon dioxide and sodium citrate. These forming result in frothing and fizzing and therefore become a lemon volcano.

Precautions:

- Adults should strictly take control of cutting.
- Do not ingest baking soda.
- Do not ingest dish soap.
- Conduct the experiment under adult supervision.

Egg shell chalk

Do you ever feel like doing something creative and out of the box? Well you are in luck because today you'll learn how to make chalks out of leftover eggshells.

Things you'll need:

- Cellophane film.
- Egg shells.
- Teaspoon of flour.
- Teaspoon of hot water.
- Two mortars (one with small grooves)
- Colour powder (for coloured chalk).
- Rubber band.

- Something to mix with.
- Bowl.
- Straws (thick).

The procedure:

Step 1: Collect big pieces of eggshell and take of the egg membrane while wet.

Step 2: Boil the eggshells in water to avoid any germs or pungent smell.

Step 3: Dry the eggshells.

Step 4: Use the mortars to crush the eggshells preferably using the mortar with small grooves first and later made finer with the other mortar.

Step 5: Mix flour and the eggshell powder together (add coloured powder for a coloured chalk).

Step 6: Add hot water to the mixture to obtain a clay like substance.

Step 7: Make small air holes in the straw and stick the cellophane film to the bottom of the straw by covering it with a rubber band. Add the mixture into the straw.

Step 8: Let the concoction dry.

Step 9: Lastly take the dried out mixture from the straw and you have yourselves perfectly working chalks.

How it works?

It all comes down to the process of mixing and drying. Once the eggshells are finely crushed, they are mixed in with water and flour to create a paste. This paste is put into a straw which has holes so that air gets released. If you want the paste to dry properly, the water it contains shouldn't just turn to vapours; it has to be completely removed from the air around them and thus air holes are made. With this the mixture dries producing chalks.

Precautions for your safety:

- Ask for adult help while using the mortars and boiling the eggshells.
- Be careful while adding hot water to the mixture (wear gloves).
- Conduct the experiment under adult supervision.

Human Sundial

In this experiment, you will learn how to make a human sundial with your very own shadow!

Things you'll need:

- Sidewalk chalk
- Notebook
- Tape measure
- Pen/pencil

The procedure:

Step 1: Go out into an open space with no shadows for example playgrounds on a sunny day.

Step 2: Write an "X" on the spot you will stand at.

Step 3: Have someone trace your shadow using sidewalk chalk at least 3 times during the day.

Step 4: (Optional): Try to write down using your chalk, the times when you trace your shadow, in your notebook describe your shadows, write down the general location of the sun and measure the lengths of your shadow.

Step 5: From your observation, formulate a hypothesis as to why the shadow changes throughout the day and year.

How it works:

It works because the sun's location in the sky will change when the Earth rotates. From this experiment, you find that the shadows are formed from a triangle set perpendicular to the base plate of a sundial. The shadow stick is known as a gnomon.

Precautions for your safety:

- Do not go out alone, have an adult accompany you.
- Do not ingest any materials involved.

Make your own rock candy

Wouldn't it be wonderful to be able to eat delicious rock candy without having to go to the store to buy it? Well with this experiment, you sure can! because we will learn how to create this mouth-watering candy at home.

Things you'll need:

- Wooden skewer
- Water
- Clothespin
- Sugar
- Tall and narrow glass.

The procedure:

Step 1: Secure the wooden skewer in the clothespin for it to hang on the inside of the glass. The wooden skewer should be hanging one inch from the bottom of the glass.

Step 2: With the help of an adult, pour 1 cup of water into a pan and boil it.

Step 3: Add ¼ cup of sugar into the water and then mix it till it dissolves. Repeat this step until more sugar cannot be dissolved.

Step 4: Remove it from the heat and give it 20 minutes to cool.

Step 5: Remove the skewer and clothespin from the glass.

Step 6: Pour the solution into the glass until it is almost full.

Step 7: Put the skewer back into it and make sure to position it in a way in which it is handing straight down and not touching the sides.

Step 8: Now you wait for your crystals to grow which might take 4 days.

How it works:

When the sugar and water are mixed, they form a very saturated solution which means the water would only be able to hold the sugar if both of them were very warm/hot. After the water cools down, the sugar starts to come out of the solution and turns back into crystals fixing itself onto the skewer.

Precautions for your safety:

- Handle tall glass with caution.
- Ask an adult to help you with the use of wooden skewers.
- Perform the experiment under adult supervision.

Homemade Play Dough

Sometimes it's simply hard to go out and purchase play dough. But don't worry, you can make your own at home!

Things you'll need:

- 2 ½ cups of flour
- 3 Tbsp. of Citric Acid
- 1 cup of salt
- 2 Tbsp. of oil
- 2 ½ cups of water

Procedure:

Step 1:   Mix salt and water.

Step 2:   Add all of the ingredients in a large saucepan.

Step 3:   Stir the mixture on low heat until you see a ball like formation in the middle of the saucepan.

Step 4:   Once a little cooled down, knead the dough for at least 3 minutes. There you have your own play dough!

Step 5:   Remember, you can add food color of choice to make play dough of different colors.

How it works:

As we know, cooking it is backed up by chemistry. A pot containing ingredients carry out many different reactions. As for our play dough, the proteins inside the flour swell up and toughed when water is added. This is because of gluten. Though when you add salt to the dough, it slows down the breaking of the protein, which then makes it malleable. That's how your play dough forms.

Precautions for your safety:

- Do not use the stove yourself, ask an adult to do that for you.
- Do not ingest the play dough.
- Perform the experiment under adult supervision.

Rainbow in a glass

Things you'll need:

- Sugar
- Water
- Food colourings
- Tablespoon
- 5 plastic cups

The procedure:

Step 1: Start by adding 1 tablespoon of sugar in the 1st cup and gradually increase the number of tablespoons of sugar in other cups (2 tablespoons in 2nd cup, 3 in 3rd cup and 4 in 4th cup). Leave the 5th cup empty.

Step 2: Mix in 3 tablespoons of water in each cup to dissolve the sugar (if not then add 4 tablespoons).

Step 3: Add a few drops of red food colouring to the first cup, yellow to the second, green to the third and blue to the fourth cup. Stir completely.

Step 4: Add ¼ of the blue coloured solution to the empty glass. Take the back of the spoon and let ½ of the green solution drip into the liquid to make a layer between them.

Step 5: Now repeat the same process with the yellow mixture but add ¾ of it to the solution.

Step 6: Finally add the red solution to the brim of the glass and you have yourselves a beautiful rainbow.

How it works:

This whole experiment depends on the densities of the solutions. The densities of the different sugar solutions are layered on top of each other to create a rainbow effect. Starting from least dense at the top to most dense at the bottom.

Precautions for your safety:

- Do not stir the solution because the solution will eventually mix due to the miscible quality of the solution.
- Gel good colouring might cause problems while mixing so it's not recommended.
- Use a narrow container for best result.
- If sugar does not dissolve heat the solution however be careful while heating it to avoid burns.

String Phone

In this experiment, you will learn how to communicate with your friends without using the expensive smart phone but instead a string phone.

Things you'll need:

- 2 cups
- String
- Sharp pencil
- Paper clip

The Procedure:

Step 1: Cut off a lengthy piece of string.

Step 2: Create one hole on the bottom side of each cup using your pencil.

Step 3: Thread your string through both of the cups and tie a knot at each end.

Step 4: Use the paperclips to hold the string in place.

Step 5: Now all that's left to do is to communicate with another person using your string phone.

How it works:

Sound waves are created when you talk into the cup which turn into vibrations on the bottom of the cup, these vibrations move along the string and turn back into sound waves when they reach the other end.

Precautions:

- Use the sharp pencil with caution.
- Conduct this experiment in the presence of an adult.

Plastic from milk

Have you ever heard that plastic can be made from milk? Well it's more than just a myth; in fact, people have been doing so for many generations! In this experiment well show you how to make your own plastic in just 30 minutes.

Things you'll need:

- A measuring cup
- Some measuring spoons
- A cup of milk

- 4 teaspoons of vinegar
- A mug
- Paper towels
- A spoon
- A microwavable container

Procedure:

Step 1: Heat the milk in the microwavable container.

Step 2: Add the milk and vinegar to the mug and stir slowly until clumps form.

Step 3: Stack some paper towels and scoop out the curds onto it by using a spoon. Be careful not to collect the liquid as well.

Step 4: Fold the paper towels to cover the curds and squeeze them so that they absorb the liquid.

Step 5: Gather all the curds into a ball.

Step 6: Your plastic is now ready! You can now create whatever you want with it and then let it sit so that it hardens

But how does it work?

Milk contains molecules of a protein called Casein. When vinegar is added, a chemical reaction takes place between the acid in the vinegar and Casein, causing the casein to unfold and form a long chain of repeating molecules (this chain is also called a polymer). This polymer is the plastic that you create.

Precautions:

- Be careful not to overheat the milk as it may boil and spill over.
- Be careful while handling the hot milk to make sure you don't spill it on yourself or burn your hands.
- Be careful with the vinegar as to not get it into your eyes.
- Carry out this experiment under adult supervision.

Milk Art

Are you bored of creating art on paper or are just not that good at it, well milk art is a

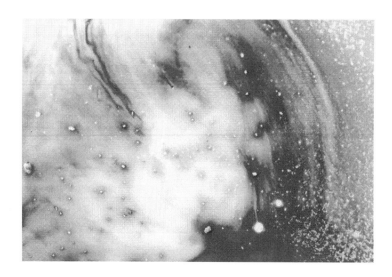

quick and fun alternative that will keep you entertained and is extremely easy to make with things already available in your kitchen?

Things you'll need:

- Milk
- Multiple Food colours
- Cotton swab
- Dish soap

- Plastic plate

The procedure:

Step 1: Place your plate on a flat surface.

Step 2: Fill your three quarters of your plate with milk.

Step 3: Add single drops of different food coloring in multiple places in the milk.

Step 4: Dip the cotton on your cotton swab in dish soap.

Step 5: Now lightly tap that end of the cotton swab on the food colouring in the milk and watch the art come to life.

How it works:

The fat in the milk acts as a layer, preventing the food coloring from sinking and dispersing and instead causing it to sit on top of it. As dish soap in its nature breaks down the oil and grease (which are fats) found on dirty dishes, it breaks down the fat in milk and enables the food color to move around and form beautiful patterns you can visibly see.

Precautions:

- Do not ingest dish soap.
- Conduct the experiment under adult supervision.

Lemon battery

In this experiment you will learn how to create electricity using a fruit!

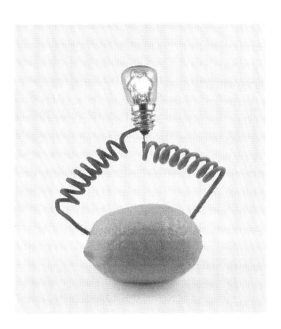

Things you'll need:

- Lemon
- Steel paper clip/ a piece of zinc
- Wire stripper
- 18 gauge copper wire
- Sandpaper

The procedure:

Step 1: Get an adult to help you out.

Step 2: Utilize the wire stripper to strip 21/2 inches of the plastic insulation off of the wire.

Step 3: Take off the piece of the stripped wire from the main roll.

Step 4: Straighten the steel paper clip and using the wire stripper again, strip it so it is the same length as your copper wire.

Step 5: Rub out any rough spots you notice in the wire and paperclip using sandpaper.

Step 6: To loosen up the lemon juice, roll the lemon on your table lightly.

Step 7: Put the copper wire 1 inch into the lemon.

Step 8: Stick your paperclip in the lemon in a location or spot where it is 1/4 inches away from the copper wire.

Step 9: Now your lemon battery is producing an electric current which can be noticed by a tingle you feel if you touch your tongue to the metal ends.

How it works:

A lemon battery is a voltaic battery which works because of an electrolyte. Electrolytes are substances which can carry electrical currents when it is dissolved in water. In this case the electrolyte works because of the sour citric acid inside the lemon juice. You can also notice it with your tongue because the salt that is in your saliva/spit makes it an electrolyte.

Precautions for your safety:

- Use the wire stripper with caution.
- Be careful around lemons, not getting the juice in your eyes.
- Perform this experiment under adult supervision.

Homemade Ice cream in a bag

Have you ever been sitting at home and wishing you had ice cream to go along with that meal you just had? Do you have a few resealable plastic bags backs sitting around? Well you're in luck, because in this experiment you'll learn how to make your own ice cream using plastic bags in just 15 minutes!

Things you'll need:

- A large bag (preferably gallon sized)
- A small bag (you can have 2 just to be safe)
- Two tablespoons of sugar
- A cup of half and half
- Half teaspoon of vanilla
- Half a cup of salt (preferably the chunky kind)
- 6 cups of ice

- An empty ice cream cone (optional)
- Toppings (optional)

Procedure:

Step 1: Add the half and half, sugar and vanilla into the smaller bag and seal it while pushing out as much air as you can. You can now seal this bag in the other similar sized bag if you like.

Step 2: Add the salt and ice into the larger bag.

Step 3: Place the smaller bag into the larger one and seal it.

Step 4: Now Shake!! Do this until the ice cream starts to thicken and is your preferred consistency.

Step 5: Now you can scoop your ice cream out into a bowl or cone and add toppings of your choice.

But how does it work?

The salt we added lowers the melting point of ice. However, the ice still needs to melt and thus absorbs heat from its surroundings such as the bag with the ingredients. Since the ice takes the heat away, the ingredients start to solidify and turn into ice cream.

Precautions:

- Be careful while shaking the bag. The bag could potentially rip and cause the ice and salt to go flying.

Pouring water into a cup without using our hands.

The following experiment is all about water and its unique properties. Most of us know that water is made up 3 atoms. Two of hydrogen and 1 of oxygen hence the formula 'H2O'.

The water has both cohesive (it can stick to itself) and adhesive (it can also stick to other things!) Properties. There might be a day when we're bored of simply pouring water from one glass to another and instead could use a simple piece of paper towel to do the work

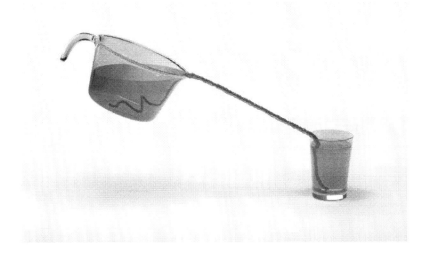

for us!

Things you'll need:

- Two cups (any material available)
- Some paper towel
- and of course, some water!

Procedure:

Step 1: Fill a cup with water only halfway.

Step 2: Place an empty cup next to it.

Step 3: Take the paper towel, twist it and put one of its ends into the cup with water and the other end into the empty cup.

Step 4: Wait!

What you will start to notice in just a few minutes is that the water will travel from the half full cup of water to the empty cup!

How it works:

It all comes down to the properties of water molecules. The atoms of hydrogen and Oxygen end up having positive and negative charges. This is why they stick to each other! Because of the property of adhesiveness, the water molecules stick to and absorb in the paper towel as well. This, in turn makes a stream which flows from the cup with water to the cup without it. Viola! You managed to pour water from one cup to another without actually using your hands.

Precautions for your safety:

- To be safe, avoid using glass cups and stick to plastic/paper cups.
- Use water at room temperature to avoid any burns.
- Conduct the experiment in the presence of an adult.

Teabag rocket

Things you'll need:

- A tea bag
- Scissors
- Lighter or matchbox
- A plate

The procedure:

Step 1: Take your scissors and cut the tip of the teabag where the string or staple is attached.

Step 2: Take the tea out of the bag to make the bag completely empty.

Step 3: Open the teabag and place it upright in a cylindrical shape on a plate.

Step 4: Use the matchbox or the lighter to burn the top rim of the tea bag and wait for the paper to turn into ash. As that is happening you can see the tea bag lift up in the air from the plate.

How it works:

There are 2 reasons for this experiment. The first one is the difference between the density of the air surrounding the cylinder and inside the tea bag cylinder. Due to the flames the air molecules inside the cylinder get heated and rise due to low density meanwhile the cooler/denser molecules in the surrounding move downwards causing the rocket to launch. This brings us to the second reason which is the generation of convection currents. The cycle of less dense air rising and denser air moving downwards continues making the tea bag shoot up in the air.

Precautions for your safety:

- Be very careful while burning the teabag.
- Conduct the experiment under adult supervision.
- Do not use a plastic plate due to a fire hazard.

Vinegar pops

Things you'll need:

- Vinegar
- Ice tray
- Baking soda
- Food colouring (for coloured popsicle)

The procedure:

Step 1:   Add vinegar and food colouring (for coloured Popsicle but optional) in the ice tray.

Step 2: Put the ice tray in a freezer and wait for 4-6 hours for it to freeze completely.

Step 3: Take the vinegar pops out of the freezer and lay it down on a plate with baking soda.

Step 4: Wait for a little while and enjoy the bubbling of the vinegar pops.

How it works?

It all comes down to the ph. scales of the ingredients. Vinegar is an acid and baking powder is a base which allows a chemical reaction to take place and releases carbon dioxide to cause the bubbling.

Precautions for your safety:

- It is edible however not recommended due to the strong acidic taste.

Quicksand

You have probably heard of quicksand before or maybe seen it in movies, but have you ever wondered what it would feel like to be in it. Well in this experiment you will make your own and experience just that, but don't worry it will not be enough to drown in.

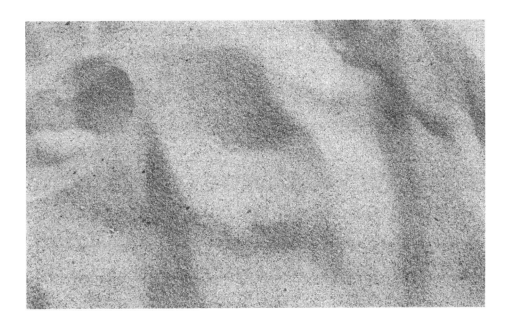

Things you will need:

- A box of cornstarch
- A few cups of water
- A mixing bowl

Procedure:

Step 1: Add the cornstarch into the bowl,

Step 2: Slowly add the water while stirring the mixture.

Step 3: Stir until it becomes a thick liquid (it should have a consistency similar to that of honey)

Step 4: Your quicksand is ready! You can now dip your hand in and try to move it around. Additionally, you can drop an object in the mixture and try to remove it. You will find that both are difficult to do.

But how does it work?

The mixture you just made, and quicksand are examples of non-Newtonian liquids, this means that its viscosity (how thick it is) changes with the amount of force applied to it. For example, if you were to step on quicksand, it would behave more like water and you would sink in. But if you were to hit it forcefully it would behave like a solid and will probably hurt.

Precautions for your safety:

- It is recommended to not ingest cornstarch or the final product.
- Perform the experiment under adult supervision.

Dyed plants

Have you ever needed to decorate your house, or wanted gift someone a flower, but just couldn't find the right color? Well no need to worry anymore, as you can dye a flower to give it any color you want! In this experiment we will show you how to do just that.

Things you will need:

- White flowers (you could use gerberas or carnations)
- A jar or cup
- Food color of your choice
- Scissors

Procedure:

Step 1: Fill the jar or cup half way with water.

Step 2: Add a few drops of food color to the water and stir lightly.

Step 3: Cut the end of the stem of the flower using the scissors.

Step 4: place the stem of the flower into the water and wait for the color to appear on the petals.

But how does it work?

Plants absorb water through their stems and transport it around their body, this is called **capillary action**. Water does not only stick to surfaces; it sticks to itself as well. This is a property of water called **cohesion**. It is why water moves up the stem of a plant in a continuous stream. Water moves up the plant, through all of its parts and then leaves the plant through it leaves or petals by **evaporating** (turning into gas), this process is called **transpiration**. Since the water we added had dye in it, this dye is transported with the water and when the water evaporated it left the dye behind on the petals. This is why the petals take on the color of the water.

Precautions for your safety:

- It is recommended to not ingest food coloring.
- Use a clear plastic glass or cup and avoid using glass.
- Perform the experiment under adult supervision.

Orange fizz

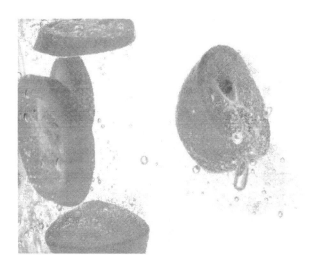

In this experiment you will learn how to make a delicious orange, bubble in your mouth.

Things you'll need:

- Orange
- Baking soda
- Knife

The procedure:

Step 1: Using a knife, cut the orange into slices.

Step 2: Dip one of the slices you cut into 1/2 teaspoon of baking soda.

Step 3: Now you can eat the slice of orange and feel it start to bubble inside your mouth.

How it works:

When the baking soda and citric acid of the orange, mix, a lot of carbon dioxide bubbles are formed.

Precautions:

- Be careful while handling the knife.
- Conduct the experiment in the presence of an adult.

Boat that runs on baking soda and vinegar

Making and playing with a paper boat gets boring but what if you could make a boat that moves by itself like it has an engine. You can do this by constructing this easy boat that runs on baking soda and vinegar at home.

 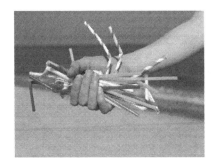 

Things you'll need:

- Small disposable plastic bottle
- Paper napkins
- Baking soda
- Plastic straw
- Vinegar
- Scissors
- Clear tape
- Large tub
- Water

The procedure:

Step 1:   Place your tub on the floor and fill it with water.

Step 2:   Take the plastic bottle and cut out a hole the size of the round edge of the straw at the bottom end of the plastic bottle.

Step 3:   Fit the straw in the hole you cut and stick the tape around it to keep the straw in its present position and to stop any air from flowing out or water from flowing in the bottle.

Step 4:   Add a small amount of vinegar into the bottle.

Step 5:   Drop a little baking soda onto the paper napkin and fold it.

Step 6:   Keep near your tub and quickly put in the napkin with baking soda into the plastic bottle and place the lid back on.

Step 7:   Put your bottle in the tub and it should start to move like a boat into the water.

How it works:

Vinegar mainly being acetic acid reacts with baking soda (sodium bicarbonate) which is alkaline in nature. As the chemical reaction between an acid and an alkali results in the production of carbon dioxide gas this is what happens when the baking soda in the napkin meets the vinegar. Carbon dioxide gas is released through the back end as the straw is the only exit for the gas. The force with which it is released causes the bottle to move forward.

Precautions:

- Cutting should be done by adults only.
- Do not ingest baking soda.

- Conduct the experiment under adult supervision.

Levitating orb

Have you ever dreamed of being a magician? Or maybe you would like to impress your friends. Well in this experiment, we are going to show you how to make an orb levitate.

Things you will need:

- A PVC pipe about 60cm long and 2.5 cm wide (this will be your magic wand)
- 6 strands of Mylar tinsel
- A fur cloth (optional)
- Scissors

Procedure:

Step 1: Place the strands of tinsel together and tie them at one end.

Step 2: Knot them at the other end at about 15 cm from the first knot

Step 3: Cut off the extra tinsel near the knots.

Step 4: Take the PVC pipe and rub it against the fur (or your hair) for about 10 seconds.

Step 5: Drop the tied-up tinsel onto the pipe. Once it touches the pipe the tinsel will start to levitate.

But how does it work?

When you rub the pipe against the fur or your hair, you give the pipe a negative static charge. The orb on the other hand, has a positive charge and since opposite charges attract the orb is initially attracted to the pipe and touches it. But once the orb touches the rod, the negative charges transfer onto the orb. Now they both have a negative charge, and since similar charges repel each other, the orb gets pushed away and thus levitates.

Precautions for your safety:

- Ask an adult to use the scissors for you.
- Do not perform the experiment without adult supervision.

Invisible ink

Growing up you've probably used invisible ink pens, well today you'll learn how to make invisible ink at home as well as learn the science behind it!

Things you'll need:

- Water
- Half lemon
- Cotton swab
- Paper (white)
- Spoon
- Bowl
- A lamp or bulb
- Lemon squeezer

The procedure:

Step 1: Using a lemon squeezer, squeeze some lemon juice into the bowl.

Step 2: Add a few drops of water to the bowl.

Step 3: Using a spoon, mix the two ingredients together.

Step 4: Take a cotton swab and dip it into the mixture.

Step 5: Use that same cotton swab to write down a message on the sheet of white paper.

Step 6: You have to wait for the juice to dry up so that the ink settles and becomes fully invisible.

Step 7: You will now be able to see the message by putting your light source close to it so that it heats up a little.

How it works:

When you dilute the lemon juice in water and put it on paper, it becomes very hard to see. Since lemon juice turns brown when heated, putting a light source near it will make the invisible message appear.

Precautions:

- Be careful when heating the paper.
- Conduct the experiment in the presence of an adult.

Your personal Edible water bottle

A plain old water bottle can get boring at times. This summer you can keep yourselves hydrated with a bottle you can also eat!

Things you'll need:

- ½ gram of sodium Alginate
- 2 ½ grams of calcium lactate
- A big bowl
- A small bowl
- Mixer
- A soup spoon
- Water

Procedure:

Step 1: In the small bowl, add ½ a gram of sodium alginate and ½ a cup of water.

Step 2: Thoroughly combine the two using a mixer. Leave the mixture out for 15 minutes. It will turn from white to clear.

Step 3: In the bigger bowl, stir the calcium lactate with 2 cups of water. Make sure to dissolve.

Step 4: Using the soup spoon, scoop up the sodium alginate mixture.

Step 5: Add the sodium alginate mixture to the calcium lactate. You will see the immediate formation of a ball of water. Now let the ball stay for 3 minutes.

Step 6: Now gently remove the ball from the calcium lactate solution and put it in a bowl of water. This will stop anymore reactions from happening.

Step 7: Gently remove the balls from the water bowl and now they are ready to be drunk from and eaten as they are algae-based polymers!

How it works:

After the sodium alginate meets calcium lactate, it starts to coagulate (gel forms) and resultantly make calcium alginate. The solution does not have a reaction with calcium lactate and therefore does not turn into gel. It leaves the center in liquid form which is the water. This way you can both drink water from the bottle and eat it as well.

Precautions for your safety:

- Perform the experiment under adult supervision.
- Perform the experiment over a sink or someplace where you can be messy.

Invisible Licorice

In this experiment you will turn yummy licorice invisible!

Things you'll need:

- Licorice
- Tall glass
- Cooking oil

The procedure:

Step 1: Add the cooking oil to the drinking glass.

Step 2: Put the licorice into the glass too.

Step 3: Position it in a way that it is leaning against the side of the drinking glass.

Step 4: Observe the side of the glass while turning it to see that the licorice starts to slowly change size and disappears.

How it works:

This is a trick of light; the oil bends the light which makes it seem as if the licorice has disappeared or turned invisible.

Precautions:

- Carefully handle the glass.
- Perform experiment under adult supervision.

Making Water Float

In this experiment you will learn how make water, float!

Things you'll need:

- Water
- Plastic cup
- Index card
- Water bucket

The procedure:

Step 1: Pour water into the plastic cup till it is ¾ full.

Step 2: Using your index card/thick piece of paper, cover the mouth of the plastic cup completely.

Step 3: Start to turn the cup upside down and while doing that hold the index card firmly so that the water does not leak, then take off your hand from the card and watch as the magic happens. (Put a bucket under the cup before doing this step in case it fails).

How it works:

The air pressure will be some both above and beneath the water so that once equal forces are applied to the opposite directions, they start to cancel each other and then gravity pulls down the water.

Precautions:

- Conduct the experiment in the presence of an adult.

Taste test

In this experiment you will learn how important smell is in order to taste.

Things you'll need:

- An apple
- Cotton ball
- Vanilla essence

The procedure:

Step 1: Put some drops of vanilla onto the cotton ball.

Step 2: Put the cotton covered by vanilla essence near your nose and eat an apple while sniffing it.

Step 3: Now you will notice how the apple tasted bitter because of the smell of the vanilla essence.

How it works:

Our sense of smell and taste are connected. ¾ of what we taste is also connected to what we smell which was the case here.

Precaution:

- Conduct the experiment in the presence of an adult.

Bouncy Egg

Eggs are used in many different cuisines around the world and can be found in so many different shapes and sizes. In this experiment we will show you our favourite kind of egg i.e. a bouncy one!!

Things you will need:

- An egg
- A cup or jar
- Vinegar

Procedure:

Step 1: Place the egg in the jar or cup without breaking it.

Step 2: Submerge the egg in vinegar.

Step 3: Leave it for a few days (1-3 should be enough).

Step 4: Remove the egg from the jar and peel the shell.

Step 5: Bounce the egg around!

But how does it work?

The vinegar slowly dissolves the shell of the egg. Once that is gone a membrane covering the egg is left behind. This layer is what makes the egg that way.

Precautions:

- Perform the experiment under adult supervision.
- Using a plastic cup instead of glass.

Skittle rainbow

Do you love rainbows? And do you have skittles laying around? Well you are in luck, because in this experiment we will show you how to make a rainbow out of skittles!

Things you will need:

- Skittles
- Water
- A white plate or bowl

Procedure:

Step 1: Align the skittles in a ring inside the plate or bowl

Step 2: Add a small amount of water (just enough to cover the base)

Step 3: Wait and watch as the rainbow forms

But how does it work?

Skittles are full of sugars and dye, so once we add the water, these two **dissolve** (mix with the liquid). And the reason the colour moves inward is due to a simple property called **diffusion**. This means that particles move from regions of higher concentrations to regions of lower concentration until they are evenly spread apart. Therefore, the colours move from the skittles (the region where there is a lot of dye) to the centre of the plate (where there is no dye).

Precautions:

- Perform experiment under adult supervision.

Coke geyser

Have you ever wanted to go on a trip to go see a geyser, but for some reason you couldn't go? Well don't worry because in this experiment we will show you how to make your own geyser using a bottle of coke.

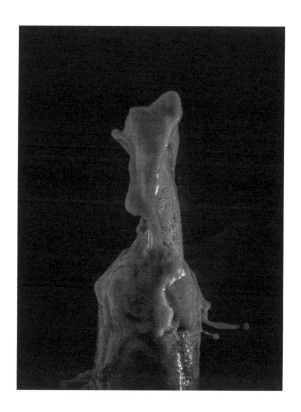

Things you will need:

- A large bottle of diet coke
- A pack of Mentos
- A funnel (optional)

Procedure:

Step 1:   Open the bottle

Step 2:   Drop about 6 Mentos into the bottle (a funnel might help with this process) and quickly take a few steps back.

Step 3:   Watch it explode!

But how does it work?

There are several theories as to how this works. The most commonly explored is that Mentos has dozens of small pores which speed up the release of carbon dioxide that is trapped in the bottle of the coke. This is because the pores give a much larger area for the reaction to take place.

Precautions:

- Do not do this experiment inside your house as it will make a mess
- Distance yourself from the bottle as the reaction will occur very rapidly

Solar Oven

Imagine this, it's a hot summer day, you feel that you could cook an egg in this heat. But did you know, that could be more than just a metaphor, because in this experiment we will show you how to use the sun to make your own solar (that means powered by the sun) oven.

Things you will need:

- A pizza box
- Scissors
- Aluminium foil
- Tape

- A Ruler
- A stick
- Plastic wrap

Procedure:

Step 1: Cut open a 3-sided flap in the lid of the box. Leave approximately 1-inch borders when you cut.

Step 2: Line the inside of the flap and the inside of the box with aluminium foil. Try to line it as smoothly as possible. You may need to use tape to stick it.

Step 3: Tape the plastic wrap across the opening you cut in the lid. Do this for both sides.

Step 4: Prop open the flap of the box using the stick

Step 5: Your oven is ready! Now you can use it to make eggs, Smores or even toast. Just remember to pre heat it first.

But how does it work?

In this experiment, we are using the aluminium to reflect the rays of the sun that are coming towards you. The flap reflects the rays into the box, where the air trapped by the plastic wrap starts to heat up. The foil inside the box does the same task; it bounces around the rays inside the box. This way the box starts to heat up and so does the food.

Precautions:

- Handle scissors with care.

- Perform the experiment under adult supervision.

Marshmallow Catapult

Have you ever wondered what times where like when catapults were still in use? Have you ever wondered how they work? Well in this experiment, we will show just that.

Things you will need:

- 4 marshmallows to build and however many you would like to launch
- 7 sticks
- Tape
- A plastic spoon
- A rubber band

Procedure:

Step 1: Make a triangle with 3 sticks and 3 marshmallows.

Step 2: Turn that triangle into a pyramid using 3 more sticks and another marshmallow.

Step 3: Place the rubber band around the topmost marshmallow.

Step 4: Tape the plastic spoon with the last remaining stick and fish the stick through the rubber band.

Step 5: Insert this stick into one of the lower marshmallows.

Step 6: Launch the marshmallows by placing them on the plastic spoon and pulling it back.

But how does it work?

Every object on this planet has **potential energy**. This is the energy stored in itself and could be used by converting it into other kinds of energy. When you pull the rubber band it has potential energy (**elastic potential energy** to be more specific) and the object that you place in the spoon also has potential energy. Once you let the spoon go, it starts to move. This means that the potential energy is converted into **kinetic energy** (which is the energy a moving object has) and this energy is then also transferred to the marshmallow thus making it fly through the air!

Precautions:

- Do not launch sharp object as someone could get hurt
- Be careful when handling the sticks as you could prick yourself or others around you
- Don't pull too hard on the spoon or the catapult could break and potentially hurt someone

Cut ice in half

Have you ever felt that your ice cubes are too big to fit in your glass? Or maybe that they take up too much space? Well in this experiment, we will explore how to cut ice cubes in half.

Things you will need:

- An ice cube
- A copper wire (or a fishing line)
- A container
- A tray
- Some weights

Procedure:

Step 1: Place the container, upside down, on the tray

Step 2: Place the ice cube on the tray

Step 3: Attach the weights to the ends of the wire

Step 4: Rest the wire on the ice so that the weights dangle on either side

Step 5: That's it! The wire should cut the ice cube in half. It may take a little while though.

But how does it work?

The thin wire applies a high amount of pressure on the ice. This lowers the melting point of ice and thus the wire starts to cut through. The same thing happens when we make snowballs! When we squeeze the snowball, the outside melts and the shape forms.

Precautions:

- Be careful with the wire as it may prick or cut you.
- Handle the weights with care as they may fall and hurt you.
- Secure the weights tightly as they could slip out.

Snow Fluff

In this experiment you will learn how to make your own fluffy snow at home to play with!

Things you'll need:

- Corn starch
- Shaving cream
- Food colouring
- Large bowl
- Spoon

The procedure:

Step 1: Add one cup of corn starch into your large bowl.

Step 2: Add one cup of shaving cream using your spoon in the bowl.

Step 3: Add a few drops of food colouring and then stir.

Step 4: After stirring, when the mixture starts to look like grated cheese, using your hands, squish the mixture.

Step 5: The mixture will soon turn into a dough textured ball which you can play with!

How it works:

Since shaving cream is made of small bubbles, their surface tension will help the particles of the corn starch stay afloat after both the ingredients mix.

Precautions:

- Do not consume the snow.
- Conduct the experiment in the presence of an adult.

Erupting Volcano

In this experiment, you will learn how to make your home made volcano erupt

Things you'll need:

- A volcano (you can ask an adult or your teacher to learn how to make a volcano out of clay or paper mache)
- A container (one that fits inside the volcano)
- Vinegar
- Liquid washing soap
- Baking soda

The procedure:

Step 1:   Take your container and put it inside the volcano.

Step 2:   Add two spoons of baking soda.

Step 3:   Pour one spoon of liquid dish washing soap.

Step 4:   Add an ounce of vinegar and now watch as your volcano erupts.

How it works:

A chemical reaction takes place when the baking soda and vinegar are mixed which creates the carbon dioxide gas. Since there is no room for the gas to properly spread out in the container, it spreads out through the opening causing an eruption.

Precautions:

- Do not consume any of the ingredients.
- Conduct the experiment in the presence of an adult.

Slime

Have you ever wondered how to make the slime you see in stores at your own home? Well in this experiment, you will learn how to make it.

Things you'll need:

- Elmer's glue
- borax powder
- water
- food colouring (your own choice of colour)
- tablespoon
- plastic spoon
- 2 small disposable cups

The procedure:

Step 1: Take one of your cups and add water to it, as well as a spoon of your borax powder, then use your spoon to stir it.

Step 2: Add glue to your other disposable cup until it is 1 inch full.

Step 3: Pour 20 ml of the water to the cup of glue then stir it.

Step 4: Add some drops of your chosen food colouring and then stir it till it is completely mixed.

Step 5: Pour 1 tablespoon of the borax solution to the glue and water mixture.

Step 6: Stir well till your slime forms and then play with it after letting it sit for a few seconds.

How it works:

Slime is made of polymers which are large chains of molecules. These molecules become tangled when the chemical reaction happens between the glue and borate ions which creates slime.

Precautions:

- Do not eat the slime.
- Conduct the experiment in the presence of an adult.

Ferromagnetic Fluid

In this experiment, you will learn how to make ferromagnetic fluid also known as Ferro fluid.

Things you'll need:

- Liquid laser printer toner
- Graduated cylinder
- Corn oil
- Glass beaker
- Neodymium magnet
- Stirrer

The procedure:

Step 1: Using your graduated cylinder, measure 50 ml of the liquid laser printer toner and then add it to the glass beaker.

Step 2: Take your corn oil and measure 30 ml of it, then pour it into the beaker.

Step 3: Using your stirrer, mix the corn oil and toner together until the solution is as homogeneous as possible.

Step 4: Take your magnet and place it outside the beaker, then watch as the magic happens.

How it works:

Ferro fluid is a liquid that has magnetic particles which come from the magnetized iron oxide it has. This allows the fluid to change shape when the magnet is placed near the beaker.

Precautions:

- Do not bring the magnet near electronics.
- Do not place your fingers between the magnet.
- Conduct the experiment in the presence of an adult.

Leak Proof Bag

In this experiment you will learn how to make a leak proof bag with just a pencil!

Things you'll need:

- Plastic bag
- Pencils
- Water

The procedure:

Step 1: Pour water into the plastic bag until it is one half full and seal the bag shut.

Step 2: Sharpen your pencils.

Step 3: Hold the top of the bag with one hand and your sharpened pencil with the other, then push the pencil through the bag, halfway out from the other side.

How it works:

Since the plastic bag is made of polymer which is long chains of molecules so when you push the pencil through it, the molecules start to spread out as well as seal themselves around the pencil.

Precautions:

- Conduct the experiment near a sink so if anything goes wrong, a mess won't be made.
- Conduct the experiment in the presence of an adult.

Moon Sand

In this experiment, you will learn how to make moon sand which is a lot of fun to play with!

Things you'll need:

- Flour
- Baby oil
- Food colouring

The procedure:

Step 1: Put 9 cups of flour into one large bowl.

Step 2: Add two tablespoons of food colouring (colour of your choice).

Step 3: After mixing up the food colouring and flour, add 1 ¼ of baby oil and mix with your hands.

Step 4: Now that your moon sand is ready, it's time to play with it!

How it works:

Moon sand is a substance that looks just like sand but can be moulded into solid shapes.

Precautions:

- Conduct the experiment in the presence of an adult.

Homemade Bouncy Ball

In this experiment you will learn how to make your very own bouncy ball to play with!

Things you'll need:

- Warm Water
- Borax
- Glue
- 2 mixing cups
- Corn starch
- Plastic spoon

The procedure:

Step 1: Add 120 ml of warm water to one of the cups and then a teaspoon of borax powder into the same cup. Using your plastic spoon, mix until the powder dissolves.

Step 2: In the other cup, add 1 tablespoon of the glue.

Step 3: Put half a teaspoon of the borax solution as well as a tablespoon of corn starch to the cup with glue in it (don't stir it).

Step 4: Let it sit for 15 seconds and then fully mix.

Step 5: When you can no longer stir the mixture, take it out and start kneading it with your hands until it solidifies. Continue kneading till it becomes smooth as well as round.

Step 6: Now your bouncy ball is ready to be played with!

How it works:

Through this activity, it is shown that the borax is like a cross linker between itself and the polymer molecules in the glue by creating long chains of molecules which will stay together rather than fall apart when picked up. The corn starch is also helpful as it secures the molecules together for them to hold their shape.

Precautions:

- Do not eat the glue or borax.
- Conduct the experiment in the presence of an adult.

Glowing Bouncy Egg

In this experiment you will learn how to make the egg-cellent glowing bouncy egg!

Things you'll need:

- Egg
- Clear glass/jar
- Vinegar
- Yellow highlighter

The procedure:

Step 1: Extract the ink out of the yellow highlighter into the clear glass.

Step 2: Add one raw egg to the glass.

Step 3: Then cover them with vinegar.

Step 4: Now all you have to do is wait 2 days till the eggshell has disintegrated.

Step 5: To see if the ball glows, shine a black light on it and you'll notice how it glows green.

How it works:

The eggshell disintegrated because of the acetic acid in the vinegar. After this the egg was able to expand and the membrane allowed a little bit of the water with the highlighter ink to pass through by a process known as osmosis which allowed the egg to glow.

Precautions:

- Do not eat the egg.
- Conduct the experiment in the presence of an adult.

Geometric Bubbles

In this experiment you will learn how to make bubbles in fun and different shapes.

(In this specific one you will learn how to make pyramid shaped bubbles)

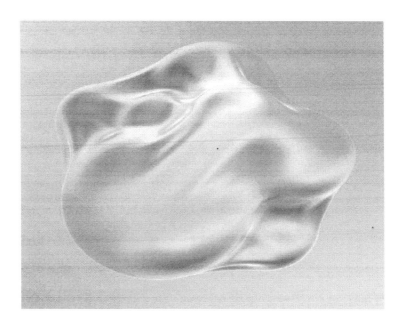

Things you'll need:

- Bubble solution
- Straight straws
- Pipe cleaners (chenille stems)

The procedure:

Step 1:   Start by cutting off each straw into half than repeat the same step to get 4 straw sections from each of them.

Step 2:   Thread the chenille stem through a straw and then bend its end to bind it.

Step 3:   Thread another 2 straws on the chenille stem.

Step 4:   To make the pipe cleaner meet the starting point, bend its long end, then twist both ends together.

Step 5:   Connect the other 2 sections of the straw to the pipe cleaner.

Step 6:   Then through one adjacent straw section, thread your chenille stem/pipe cleaner.

Step 7:   To form a pyramid, add the last straw section and then curve/bend it back to the straw joints.

Step 8:   Finally, to bind everything together, thread the pipe cleaner through an adjacent straw section.

How it works:

You are basically making a mould through the straws and pipe cleaner so that the bubble will form in the shape that you make it.

Precautions:

- Do not drink the bubble solution.
- Conduct the experiment in the presence of an adult.

Magic Finger Pepper

You will be learning about surface tension through this simple experiment known as magic finger pepper!

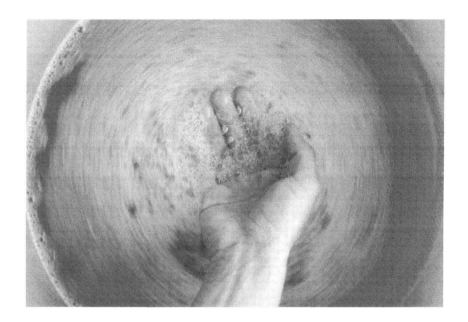

Things you'll need:

- Dish washing soap
- A bowl
- Water
- Pepper

The procedure:

Step 1:   Fill half the bowl up with water.

Step 2:   Add enough pepper so that it covers the top of the water.

Step 3:   Dip the top of your finger in the dish washing soap and touch the water in the middle then watch as the magic happens!

How it works:

By soap touching the water, the surface tension will change, and the pepper will not float on the top anymore either but the water molecules in order to keep the surface tension will pull back from where the soap is and take the pepper along.

Precautions:

- Conduct the experiment in the presence of an adult.

Straw Airplane/Hoop Glider

You've probably made paper airplanes, but have you ever made straw airplanes? Well today's the day! In this experiment you will learn how to make an airplane out of straws.

 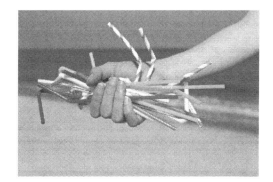

Things you'll need:

- Plastic straw
- Tape
- Scissors
- 3 x 5 index card

The procedure:

Step 1: Snip the index card into 3 different pieces each measuring 1 inch by 5 inches

Step 2: In a hoop, tape two of the pieces of the index card together.

Step 3: Using the last piece of the index card, make another hoop.

Step 4:   Tape the hoops at each end of the straw.

Step 5:   Now you can fly your airplane by throwing it in the air similar to how you throw a dart.

How it works:

The hoops balance the straw. The bigger one creates air resistance so that it stays on level and the smaller helps to avoid it going off course.

Precautions:

- Conduct the experiment in the presence of an adult.

Dry Ice Crystal Bubble

In this experiment, you will learn how to make crystal bubbles.

Things you'll need:

- Bowl (smooth rim and smaller than 12 inches in diameter)
- Tablespoon
- Dawn liquid dish soap
- Water
- Plastic cup
- Cloth
- Gloves

- Dry ice

The procedure:

Step 1: Add 2 tablespoons of liquid dish soap and 1 tablespoon of water into the plastic cup.

Step 2: Cut the cloth into a strip, 2.5cm wide and 46cm long.

Step 3: Soak the strip of cloth into the soap solution you made earlier and make sure it is fully submerged.

Step 4: Fill the bowl with warm water till it is half full.

Step 5: Wear your gloves and transfer a few pieces of the dry ice to the bowl so that enough fog is formed.

Step 6: Now remove the strip of cloth from the solution also remove any excess soap. Stretch the cloth out by your hands and pull it along the wet rim of the bowl. A soap film should form.

How it works:

The gas that is formed by combining carbon dioxide and water vapour is a cloud of water droplets. The soap film traps the cloud into a giant bubble creating a crystal bubble.

Precautions:

- Do not lick or touch the dry ice with your bare hands.
- Conduct the experiment in the presence of an adult.

Magic Mud

In the experiment you will learn how to make fun magic mud to play with!

Things you'll need:

- Corn starch
- Water
- Food colouring
- Bowl
- Spoon

The procedure:

Step 1:   Add two cups of corn starch and one cup of water to your bowl.

Step 2:   Add a few drops of the food colouring of your choice to the bowl.

Step 3:   Mix the following ingredients with your hands or a spoon.

Step 4:   Now play with your magic mud!

How it works:

By mixing the corn starch and water, a mud textured substance is created which is safe and fun to play with!

Precautions:

- Conduct the experiment in the presence of an adult.

Ooblek

In this experiment you will learn how to make some fun ooblek.

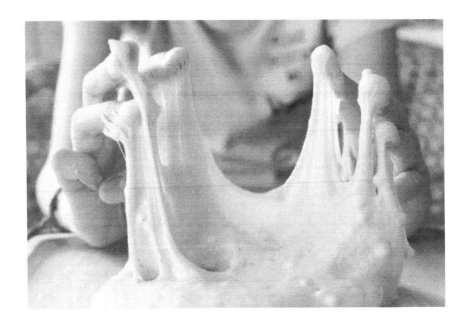

Things you'll need:

- Corn starch
- Water
- Food colouring
- Bowl
- Spoon

The procedure:

Step 1:   Add a cup of water to the bowl.

Step 2:   Slowly add 1.5 cups of corn starch to the water and mix with a spoon and then your hands.

Step 3:   Add food colouring of your own choice and mix.

Step 4:   Now your ooblek is ready to be played with.

How it works:

Ooblek is also known as a non newtonian liquid. The grains of starch are spread out in the water not dissolved. The make up of the corn starch grains causes it to hold its own shape when pressure might be applied.

Precaution:

- Conduct the experiment in the presence of an adult.

Glitter Germs

This experiment will help you learn the importance of washing your hands. (conduct this with the help of friends).

Things you'll need:

- Glitter
- Hand lotion
- Paper towels

The procedure:

Step 1: Put some hand lotion on your hands and rub it over them

Step 2: Sprinkle a little bit of glitter on your hands and rub it evenly.

Step 3:   One person should clean their hands with paper towel, while the other should wash their hands with cold water and another with warm water.

How it works:

Through this you will be able to understand germs will spread unless you wash your hands.

Precaution:

- Conduct the experiment in the presence of an adult.

Mold on bread

In this experiment you will learn the importance of washing hands by growing mold on bread.

Things you'll need:

- Bread
- Water
- Plastic zipper bag
- Masking tape

The procedure:

Step 1: Sprinkle a little bit of the water on the bread slice.

Step 2: Take out your plastic bag and put the bread in it, then seal the bag.

Step 3: Tape the sealed bag.

Step 4: Put the bread in a warm place for 7 days where it will remain undisturbed.

Step 5: In the end you will notice the moldy bread which you should immediately throw away after observing.

How it works:

The bread starts to rot over time.

Precautions:

- Do not eat the moldy bread.
- Conduct the experiment by the permission and in presence of an adult.

Salt Crystal Feathers

In this experiment you will learn how to make colourful feathers out of salt.

Things you'll need:

- Faux Colourful goose feathers.
- Morton salt
- Mason jars
- Clothespin

The procedure:

Step 1: Fill your mason jar with water. Put that water into a pot and add salt to it then boil it till the salt dissolves. Continue to add the salt till a layer of crystallized salt forms in the pot on the boiling water.

Step 2: Now add the salty water back into the jar.

Step 3: Hold the end of the feather with your clothespin to hang it over the jar.

Step 4: Dip the faux feather into the salty water and set it near a place where the sun is shining such as a window.

Step 5: Leave the feather in the water for 3 days to completely crystallize, then remove the feather from the water and set it aside to dry for a night. The next day your beautiful crystal feathers will be ready.

How it works:

Due to a very high concentration of salt in the water, the salt starts to crystallize. After the water will evaporate, the salt sticks around the feather and eventually creates salt crystals around it.

Precautions:

• Conduct the experiment in the presence of an adult.

Cloud in a Jar

In this experiment you will create your very own cloud in a jar!

Things you'll need:

- Jar (with lid)
- Hot water
- Hairspray
- Ice

The procedure:

Step 1: Pour 1/3 cup of water into the jar.

Step 2: Turn the lid of the jar upside down and put on the top part of the jar.

Step 3: Put some ice cubes on the lid and let it set for 20 seconds.

Step 4: Now take off the lid and quickly spray some hair spray into the jar, then put the lid back again with ice still on the top.

Step 5: When there is a good amount of condensation, remove the lid and watch as the cloud forms and goes into the air.

How it works:

The water vapour from the warm water meets the cool air created by the ice cubes and condenses on to the hairspray forming a cloud.

Precautions:

- Be careful with the warm water.
- Conduct the experiment in the presence of an adult.

LISA WATTS

Green Pennies

In this experiment you will learn how to turn pennies green.

Things you'll need:

- Salt
- Vinegar
- Shallow tray
- Pennies
- Paper towels/tissue

The procedure:

Step 1: Soak one paper towel into the white vinegar and line the bottom part of the tray.

Step 2: Put the pennies on top of the tissue paper and sprinkle a little bit of salt on them.

Step 3: Let the pennies sit till they slowly start to turn a green colour.

How it works:

Pennies oxidize but do not rust, instead they get covered with a green coating. By adding the white vinegar and salt, the oxide layer of the penny will start to dissolve, and the copper atoms will start to mix with the oxygen and chlorine from air and salt.

Precaution:

- Conduct the experiment in the presence of an adult.

Crystal Egg Geodes

In this experiment you will learn to make some pretty crystal geodes out of eggshells.

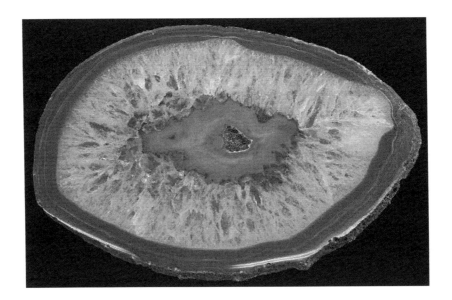

Things you'll need:

- Empty eggshells.
- Scissors
- Glue
- Paint brush
- 6 tablespoons of alum per each colour.
- 2 plastic cups
- Easter egg dyes
- Cup filled with hot water

- Bowl
- Spoon
- Paper towels
- Gloves (to avoid getting your hands coloured by the dye)

The procedure:

Step 1: Split the eggshells into two parts with the help of your scissors.

Step 2: Add a little bit of glue into the eggshells.

Step 3: Using your paintbrush, spread the glue and then add the alum crystal powder all over the glue. Now let this dry for some hours.

Step 4: Put the eggshells inside a cup each and the cut side should be up.

Step 5: Put water that is hot enough to make the alum solution super saturated, into the bowl.

Step 6: Add your colour dye to the water making it a pretty colour.

Step 7: Add 6 tablespoons of alum powder to the bowl and stir it along the way so that the alum dissolves.

Step 8: Now add half of the alum solution over the eggs and let it sit for 15 or more hours.

Step 9: Finally take out the eggs from each cup using a spoon and put them on a paper towel to dry and you've got your pretty geodes!

How it works:

The solution becomes super saturated and when it is cooled, the water loses energy. The crystals from the solution have to become a solid again because of that and because of evaporation, the crystal get to grow larger than they originally were.

Precautions:

- Do not eat the crystal egg geodes.
- Conduct the experiment in the presence of an adult.

Carbon Sugar Snake

In this experiment you will learn how to make an interesting carbon sugar snake.

Things you'll need:

- Pie tin
- Baking soda
- Sand
- Lighter

- Powdered sugar
- Small mixing bowl
- Ethanol

The procedure:

Step 1: In your bowl, add 4 teaspoons of powdered sugar and 1 teaspoon of baking soda.

Step 2: Completely fill the tin with the sand and create a mound in the middle then use your knuckles to make an indent.

Step 3: Put the ethanol in the mound and the indent in the sand fully soaking it.

Step 4: Using a spoon add the mix of sugar and baking soda to the mound.

Step 5: Now it's time to light the sand close to the sugar mixture and slowly your snake will start to form.

How it works:

When the sugar burns, a chemical reaction takes place and the sugar that doesn't burn starts to go through thermal decomposition and the baking soda also starts to decompose in the in the heat so together these reactions create the snake.

Precautions:

- Do not eat any of them ingredients.
- Be careful when using the lighter.

- Conduct the experiment in the presence of an adult.

Mummified Sausage

In this experiment you will learn how to mummify a sausage.

Things you'll need:

- Gloves
- Hot dogs
- Paper towels
- Airtight plastic storage box
- Baking soda

The procedure:

Step 1: On the bottom of the box, put 2.5 cm of the baking soda.

Step 2: Put the sausage on top of it and then put more baking soda on top of the sausage and on the sides of it.

Step 3: Close the box with the lid so that it is tightly sealed and put it away in a location where there is shade.

Step 4: After 14 days, observe how the hot dog has become mummified then throw out the hot dog along with the baking soda.

How it works:

The hot dog starts to smell bad, change colour and also shrinks because the baking soda absorbs moisture from the hot dog, desiccating.

Precautions:

- Do not eat the hot dog.
- Conduct the experiment in the presence of an adult.

Floating tennis ball

In this experiment you will learn how to make a tennis ball, float.

Things you'll need:

- Plastic storage tub
- Water
- Tennis ball

The procedure:

Step 1: Fill the plastic storage tub with water.

Step 2: Put a tennis ball in it and observe how it starts to float.

How it works:

The tennis ball is hollow, so it's filled with air which means it has less density than water which allows it to float.

Precaution:

- Conduct the experiment in the presence of an adult.

Conclusion

Science is all around us. From the food we eat to the chores we do; everything is based off of principles of physics, chemistry and biology. Since it has such a huge impact on our daily lives, it is important that we learn it and have some understanding of it. What's better than to do it ourselves? Using simple household items to understand complex scientific processes. This book was created to help you kill boredom while being productive at the same time!

These fun experiments will not only help you get better at general science but give you an opportunity to bond with your friends and family while performing the experiments. The lessons you have learnt from the sections of this book will go a long way. Next time you see a lemon, you wouldn't just think of lemonade, you'll think of all the ways you could turn it into a battery. If you don't have the money or time to go to the market and buy play dough/slime, you could simply ask your parents to take you to the kitchen and help you make your own. You wouldn't need to spend loads of money buying toys at expensive toy stores and instead you could build your own bouncy balls and hoop gliders! You'll create and learn at the same time.

Made in United States
Orlando, FL
05 November 2022

24239129R00100